IMAGES OF ENGLAND

BROADMEAD

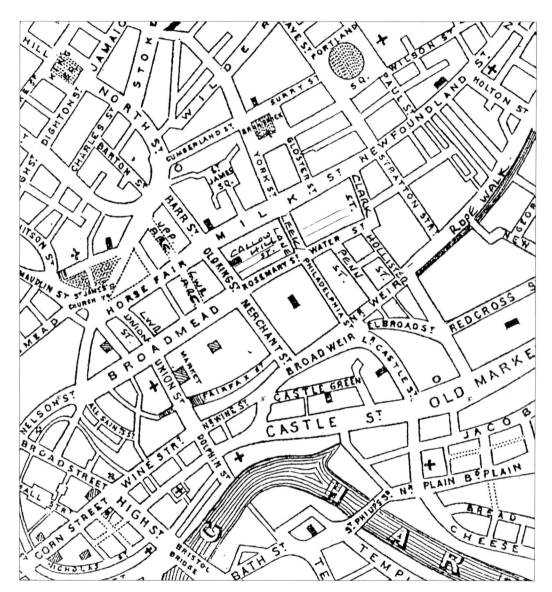

Street Layout for the Broadmead area before the new shopping development in the 1950s.

IMAGES OF ENGLAND

BROADMEAD

MIKE HOOPER

TEMPUS

I would like to dedicate this book to my late father Jim Hooper, who started my interest in the subject by showing me the changes that were happening in the early 1950s. I wish I had taken more notice then.

First published 2004

Tempus Publishing Limited
The Mill, Brimscombe Port,
Stroud, Gloucestershire, GL5 2QG
www.tempus-publishing.com

British Library Cataloguing in Publication Data.
A catalogue record for this book is available from the British Library.

ISBN 0 7524 3382 2

Typesetting and origination by Tempus Publishing Limited.
Printed in Great Britain.

Contents

The City Planner's model for the new Broadmead, late 1940s. The completed shopping centre would be built along very similar lines, unlike that shown for the Castle Park area to the left, which failed to materialize.

Acknowledgments

I would like to acknowledge the following people who have helped me in the making of this book:

Fred Searle, who had the foresight to regularly take his camera to work in the 1950s and 1960s and to record the changing face of the area, especially around Milk Street and Fairfax Street. His collection of slides, mostly unseen for the past fifty years is an invaluable source of information for the student and casual observer alike of Bristol's ever-vanishing street scenes.

Andrew Keen for allowing me access to his family's photograph albums of Bristol from over the past seventy-five years. Without these, the record of subtle changes that have taken place in the city would be hugely deficient.

Mike Barnfield, managing director of Mickleburgh's in Stokes Croft for letting me look at their archives, a yet to be appreciated goldmine of information.

The Bristol Record Office for supplying photographs from a very wide range of sources and without whom a book of this kind would be impossible.

Mr and Mrs Osbourn for supplying a family photograph.

Linda, Dominic and Natalie for extra last minute help.

Roger Angerson and Barry Williamson for information on St James' Sqaure.

And a special thanks to Veronica Smith for typing up the text and checking the context and without whom the book wouldn't have started.

Introduction

Bristol's Broadmead shopping centre, a post-war development, is about to undergo a £500 million transformation. This book sets out to show, however, that before the 1950s and '60s buildings we see today, there existed a community of people living among the tightly interwoven shops, churches, public houses and many businesses. The community was to undergo dramatic changes, not only because of the Blitz, but also because of major, planning decisions made in the light of what was then the latest in post-war thinking.

The shopping centre we know today is called Broadmead and is quite extensive. The area which I will cover in this book will be similar, and I have taken as my boundaries: the Haymarket; St James' Barton; St James' Square; York Street; Penn Street; Broad Weir; Dolphin Street and the Pithay. I do, however, remind the reader that originally Broadmead only referred to the street of that name, which ran between Nelson Street and Merchant Street.

The district covered in this book developed to the north of the old city walls surrounding the castle mound. It was a low-lying spot alongside the river Frome, which acted as part of the city's defences. The name Broadmead would seem to imply a broad meadow perhaps abutting a river, but it has been suggested that the name derives from the medieval term *brod-medes*, a wide cloth that was apparently manufactured here – I leave it up to the reader to determine which!

Numerous churches, chapels and monastic houses were established here from the later Middle Ages, the oldest being St James' Benedictine Priory, from 1129. This priory was important as it controlled the site on which the annual St James' Fair was held, and from which it would have received a considerable regular income. A friary for the Franciscans was nearby in Lewins Mead and yet another in the Broadmead/ Rosemary Street location for the Black Friars or Dominicans. Their priory was one of only a handful of ancient buildings to survive both bombs and planners in the twentieth century.

Some of the very ancient street lines survived from the early fifteenth century (e.g. Rosemary Street) right up until the present day, although their names may have changed. Development continued gradually, timber buildings being erected and quite a number of these from the early seventeenth and eighteenth centuries survived until the 1940s and '50s.

The more northerly part of the district proved to be popular for later growth as it was not so prone to flooding and was also within easy reach of the city. The late seventeenth century saw William Penn (of Pennsylvania fame) purchase land to the north of Narrow Weir for the laying out of streets along which he built houses.

In the eighteenth century virgin fields were purchased and built upon in a planned grid system, hence we had the laying out of three magnificent squares – Brunswick, Portland and St James'. We will look at the last later in the book in detail as it was inhabited by several important and interesting residents.

The houses that existed between the shops, chapels etc., were not the imposing dwellings, as in St James' Square, but lowly cottages for the working man, although they were built in the same era. They were often spread over three storeys, but perhaps with only one or two rooms on each floor. It was very common for them to be overcrowded with two, three, four or even more families – consisting of maybe eighteen tenants altogether. This practice continued right up to the point when the houses were removed in the slum-clearance scheme of the 1930s.

Due to the large number of various properties – not just houses – the constricted sites, and lack of any wish to improve conditions, meant that squalid housing continued without (as happened in other parts of the city) the building of the so-called Bye-Law houses of the 1880s onwards, so Broadmead missed out.

The large population that existed here serviced the many industries, great and small, which were within walking distance of their homes. Perhaps the largest of these was Fry's the cocoa manufactory in Union Street and the Pithay. This was started in Narrow Wine Street in 1728 and went on to become a massive concern employing, even by the end of the nineteenth century, some 1,100 people. At the top of Union Street was the large company, which would probably be called a pharmaceutical business today, of Ferris, established in 1745. There were also lesser employers, but they covered a very wide range of industries. For instance, there were brass foundries in Ellbroad Street, brushes of all kinds were made by Jones' in Mary le Port Street; cutlery in Dolphin Street – the firm of Plum's; Uriah Alsop's, in Broadmead – cabinet makers, Clarkes' wholesale clothiers in Milk Street; Carver & Sons on Castle Green – hats; Mardon, Son & Hall had an early printing works in Milk Street and produced paper bags there; mineral waters were bottled in Milk Street by W. Summers and by King's in York Street – the list is extensive.

For the population's religious needs, churches and chapels abounded, some extremely large, coping with up to 800 of the local congregation, e.g. St Peter's; the Methodist chapel in Milk Street – 620, the Friends' Meeting House – 750 and the Tabernacle in Penn Street – 800.

The need for entertainment seems to have been mostly satisfied by the large number of public houses in practically every street, but there were some early cinemas and theatres, e.g. the Gem Electric Theatre in Broad Weir and, of course, the Odeon, Broadmead, which opened on the site of one of Fry's old offices in 1938.

From 1940, all this was to change. In the first blitz on 24 November in that year Castle Street, until then Bristol's main shopping centre, was badly damaged, only to be totally destroyed in follow-up raids. The shopkeepers wanted to open, even temporarily, on their old sites, but this would not have been a long-term viability. The decision to form a new centre on a larger, flatter site nearby was not popular with the shopkeepers and other traders, but despite this, the decision was made in 1944 by the planning committee that a new Broadmead should be built.

As will be seen by the photographs collected from numerous sources for this book, it meant that hundreds of interesting buildings – churches, shops and housing – were to be removed, road lines changed and a completely different way of life introduced.

Mike Hooper
July 2004

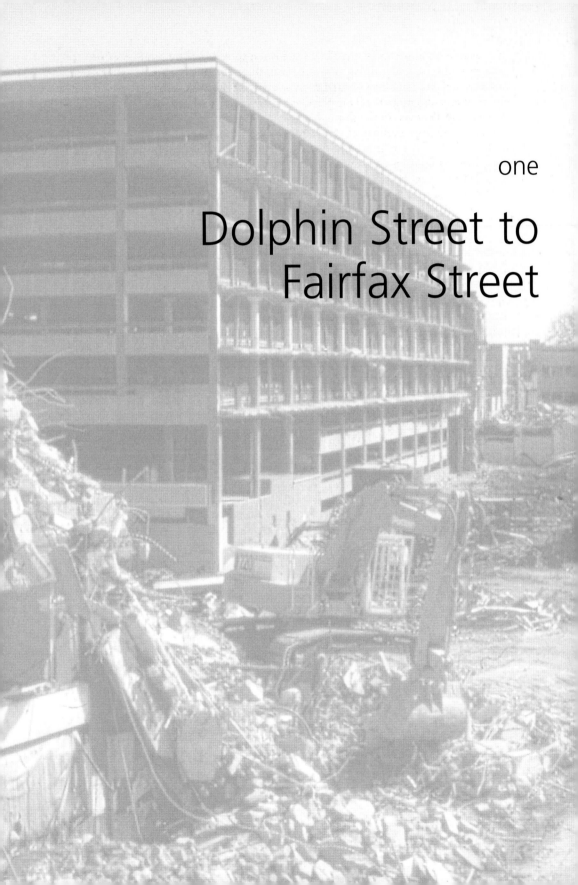

one

Dolphin Street to Fairfax Street

Our virtual walk around the district begins within what was once the medieval castle walls, in Dolphin Street. It was one of Bristol's shortest and most ancient streets, but became very important as part of the shopping centre, along with Castle Street, until destroyed in the 1940 blitz. In the 1920s, shops here included: Alexandre Ltd, tailors; George Plum, cutlers and Michael and Bailey, jewellers. There was also a large hotel. After the war the remains of these buildings' basements were cleared away and became part of a massive car park until the 1970s.

When the tidying of Castle Park was undertaken in the 1990s, the ancient well of St Edith, 1474, a major water supply to the castle inhabitants, was discovered on the corner of what was then Peter Street.

Narrow Wine Street led down from Dolphin Street to Castle Mill Street and Castle Green junction. The old buildings, many houses which had been converted to shops, were removed for the construction of Fairfax House. Industry, for instance, Stephens & Hookins' (paper bag makers) property was adjacent to these homes. Other businesses were: Joseph Merrett, umbrella maker; Eastmans', wire workers and W.B. Harris, printing works. Matthew Wansborough lived in No.3. Narrow Wine Street – he was a rival of James Watt in his application of the crank and flywheel to the steam engine in the eighteenth century.

Fairfax Street, named after Thomas Fairfax, Commander in Chief of the Roundheads in the Civil War and who captured Bristol Castle in 1645, was built over the curved course of the River Frome, along the Merchant Street to Pithay section. The natural ground level here is some 40 ft below where the castle was built and, with the walls on top, would have proved a formidable obstacle to attackers.

The building of Fairfax House in the 1950s and '60s unfortunately required the excavation of all this area and much of Bristol's history was lost. The Co-op building lasted until 1988 when it too was removed for the new Galleries Shopping Centre.

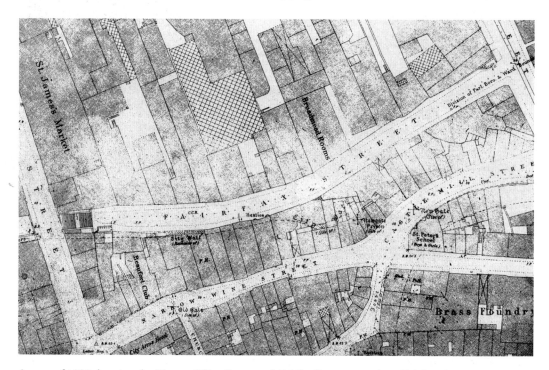

A map of 1883 showing the Narrow Wine Street and Fairfax Street area where Fairfax House was built.

The old inn, the Dolphin, from which Dolphin Street derives its name, but prior to this, Dolphin Street was called Defence Lane. The early Baptists used to meet here.

Celebrations for the opening of the Royal Edward Docks, Avonmouth, Dolphin Street, 1908. This view is from the top of Bridge Street to the top of Union Street. In the middle distance, left, is Mary le Port Street and right, Peter Street. In the 1920s George Plum made cutlery and scissors at No. 6.

A view from Bridge Street to Mary le Port Street, 1950s. At this time most of the street and church had been destroyed and the rubble cleared away. The foreground basements were to become car parks for over twenty years, before reconstruction started.

Dolphin Street to Union Street, 1959. Peter Street is off to the right, in front of the two policemen. The picturesque buildings and the bustle on the street, seen in the earlier photograph have long since disappeared. The chimney belongs to Fry's chocolate factory near the Pithay – its days were numbered.

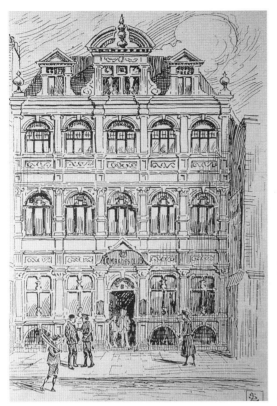

Left: Narrow Wine Street, the Comrades Club as Loxton saw it in around 1905, near its junction with Union Street.

Below: The lower part of Narrow Wine Street was cleared away in the early 1950s for the building of Fairfax House. The shops include at No.3, an early tiny Halfords, when they were mainly cycle accessory dealers. Opposite, out of the picture, was another cycle dealer who went on to bigger things – Currys, who were at Nos 31 and 32.

The old walls have been cleared; shops, houses and other buildings of Narrow Wine Street (behind the fencing) have gone and the site levelled for Fairfax House, January 1953. The top of the News Theatre is just visible over the fence.

Fairfax Street (Fairfax House was to be built on the left) from Merchant Street looking towards St Stephen's and All Saints churches, which are in the background. The odd structure on the right appears to be a gents' urinal, which is even shown on an 1883 map.

Left: This view along Fairfax Street to St Stephen's church is impossible to see today because of the Galleries Shopping Centre that covers the whole of this area. On the left, in front of the pedestrian, can be seen the site of the ancient walls that defended the castle area. The difference in height from the river, well below street level, and the top of the castle mound is very apparent here, indicating the excellent defendable position of the medieval castle. This change in level is not so easy to appreciate with the modern street layout. The building on the right is the Church Army Hostel for Men.

Below: The scaffold and sheeting form a temporary Union Street bridge, seen here from Fairfax Street. On the right, is the original arching over the River Frome, above which was built Union Street.

This view is from Narrow Wine Street across Fairfax Street (in the foreground) through to the north side of Broadmead, which can be seen in the middle distance. Smarts Bros Ltd at Nos 86 and 88 Broadmead are still there awaiting demolition. The spire of the Welsh Baptist church in St James' Barton appears over the top of Smarts Bros' property. The steelwork to the right in Broadmead is for the new Freeman Hardy and Willis.

Fairfax Street from Union Street bridge, early 1953. The curve of the road surface constructed over the river Frome has yet to be completed, but Woolworths, one of the first major stores to be built in the new Broadmead Shopping Centre is already open for business. The position of the old city defences can be seen on the right where a start has yet to be made to clear the site for Fairfax House.

Fairfax House from the tall offices in Wine Street. Every building, structure and original land surface has been removed from the Fairfax House 'island'. Some of the foundations for Fairfax House are in, the low-rise colonnaded shops have been built and opened and the Church Army hostel, adjacent, towers over them. Above the hostel can be seen Penn Street Tabernacle, awaiting demolition, and the cleared site of Broad Weir and Merchant Street, *c.* 1959.

Fairfax House – the structure begins to rise, starting from the Merchant Street end.

Left: The building of Fairfax House quickly moves on alongside a newly straightened and widened Narrow Wine Street, now known as Newgate, to align with Broad Weir where the canopies of the new shops can just be glimpsed beyond the scaffolding, *c.* 1960. The new shops, in the distance facing the camera, are on the corner of Lower Castle Street and Narrow Weir, obliterating the line of Ellbroad Street. They have yet to be let, but Keith Poples and Broadmead Wireless were to occupy two of the shops. However, demolition, even for them, was not too far distant.

Below: Newgate from Union Street. To the right is the white gable of the Bear and Rugged Staff public house, next to the Cat and Wheel on the junction of Castle Green and Little Peter Street. The tall building behind it is the rear of the old Co-op in Castle Street, *c.* 1961.

Right: Fairfax House from Narrow Wine Street (now Newgate), 1959. The archway to the bridge that led to the massive multi-storey car park takes shape.

Below: A view of Fairfax House 1959 from the Fairfax Street side; the bridge leading into the car park is yet to be built.

Fairfax House is nearly complete in 1961, and the construction of the bridge to the multi-storey car park over the shops can be seen to the left.

Not even modern buildings last forever! The view is again from Union Street bridge along Fairfax Street, but Fairfax House has been demolished, the low-rise shops are gone (Woolworths was soon to follow) to make way for the building of the Galleries Shopping Centre, April 1988.

two

Castle Green to Broad Weir

ARTHUR MAIDEN LTD.

DOWN WITH GUINNESS

YOU'LL FEEL BETTER!

In the previous chapter our walk took us along Fairfax Street and up the steps to Union Street and the St Peter's church area. Here, between the church and the river, stood St Peter's Hospital. It was a magnificently decorated timber-framed building, facing the church; its elevation to the river less so. The building probably dated back to the fifteenth century and was later lived in by Thomas Norton, who was said to be the most skilful alchemist of his time. He sold it, in 1580, to the Newton family of Barr's Court. Robert Chambers owned it for a short time, in 1602, before selling it to Robert Aldworth, a rich merchant. In 1688 Edward Colston took over the sugar refinery established there. In the time of William III, when it was the Bristol mint, it produced coinage to the value of £40 million! From 1698 it became the property of the Incorporation of the Poor, or Guardians of the Poor.

On 11 July 1832 there was a terrible outbreak of cholera just down river on the Frome. By 10 August that year, seventy-three people had died. The following day the occupants of St Peter's Hospital, which housed the infirmary of the Guardians, also became victims of the disease. There were 600 paupers there in very overcrowded conditions including fifty-eight girls sleeping in ten beds and seventy boys in eighteen beds. By the following day thirty-one had died. Some ten years later young William Budd, joined the infirmary as a doctor and later went on to become famous for his research into showing that cholera was caused by the contamination of drinking water by human waste.

To the front of St Peter's church was the News Theatre, a little cinema established in 1933, but demolished in 1956. The building began life as the Queen's Picture House, in 1910, as Bristol's first purpose-built cinema and one boasting a sliding roof to let the smoke out.

From the News Theatre our walk takes us down Little Peter Street past the two public houses – the Bear and Rugged Staff and the Cat and Wheel, and past the large Victorian St Peter's church hall. Opposite, where Castle Mill Street begins, was sited the notorious Newgate Gaol, part of the medieval castle complex. The whole street of shops and houses disappeared for the building of Fairfax House.

At the bottom of the hill we approach Broad Weir, which is not readily recognisable as the course of the River Frome, but did mark the line of the outer walls of the city and was also the quarter occupied by a large Jewish population.

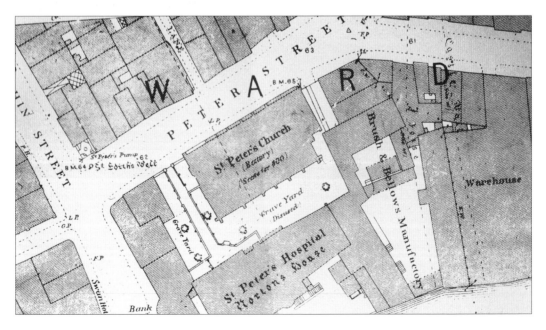

The Guardians of the Poor outside St Peter's Hospital, which was used as their main meeting place. The Incorporation of the Poor was constituted in 1696 by the election of four ratepayers from each of twelve wards and they were called the Guardians of the Poor, who were chosen to serve for four years. The mayor and twelve aldermen were also members of the court, along with any honorary Guardians who might be elected from those who contributed £100 or more to the poor fund, making the total number of Guardians seventy-nine.

Opposite: The map of 1883 showing the position of St Peter's Hospital between St Peter's church and the River Avon.

Left: A drawing of St Peter's Hospital, situated between St Peter's church and the river was once owned by Robert Aldworth in 1607 and the ornate frontage was built for him. In 1666 it became the first sugar refinery in Bristol. In 1695 it was the Bristol Mint but three years later it was taken over as a workhouse for the poor. Sadly it was bombed during the Blitz; a great loss to Bristol's architectural heritage.

Below: The News Theatre – Peter Street – opposite St Peter's church and on the corner of Little Peter Street, 1953. The Bear and Rugged Staff and Cat and Wheel public houses are to the right. The cinema showed continuous programmes and in the 1950s was one place where numerous cartoons could be watched, as television was yet to become common in people's living rooms.

From Peter Street to Little Peter Street and Narrow Wine Street, 1961. The two public houses can be seen just hanging on to the last few months of their lives. The brash new post-war era is represented by the modern face of Fairfax House on the left.

The Bear and Rugged Staff and the Cat and Wheel (rebuilt) on the corner of Little Peter Street (right) and Castle Green, 1961. Narrow Wine Street is in the foreground.

Left: The original Cat and Wheel was a half-timbered building.

Below: St Peter's church hall, Castle Green is seen here off to the right. Buildings on the left are in Castle Mill Street (a continuation of Little Peter Street) and the corner of Merchant Street can just be glimpsed between the hall and the four-storey building, which was Jay's shop.

The junction of Castle Mill Street and Narrow Wine Street before it was widened. New shops in the distance are on the Merchant Street and Broad Weir corner, which was nearing completion at this time. The view is from practically the same position as the previous photograph.

A drawing of the notorious Newgate Gaol that stood in the angle between Castle Mill Street and Fairfax Street. Mention is made of it as early as 1148 and it was rebuilt in 1691. John Howard, who visited it in 1775, described it as 'white without and foul within'. The prisoners were allowed to hand out a basket into which passers-by dropped their doles which were gifts of bread or other food, and from which we got the expression 'on the dole'. In 1615, prisoner Phelps, a fellmonger (a dealer in animal skins), was pressed to death, but it is not recorded why he received this punishment. In 1736 Joshua Harding and John Newnham were hanged, but when cut down and placed in coffins both came to life. The prison was abandoned in 1820 when the gaol on the New Cut was built.

Right: Numbers 15-18 Castle Mill Street, opposite the site of Newgate Gaol. The shops awaiting demolition are Salanson's, opticians, in the three-storey building and the smaller one to the right and Martin's fish shop. St Peter's church hall is just visible to the far right. The two buses are making their way along Broad Weir from Lower Castle Street towards Merchant Street.

Below: Jay's furnishing stores (as seen on p. 26) at the bottom of Castle Mill Street advertising 'smashing reductions', probably in readiness to clear the shop before demolition. The 1930s' car is about to go into Merchant Street, just before the turning for Fairfax Street.

Opposite above: View from the bottom of Castle Mill Street along Broad Weir, where demolition of the old shops appears to have started, to Lower Castle Street where the double decker bus can be seen at the very edge of this picture, 1957. Briton's Furnishers Ltd is on the corner of Merchant Street and still appears to be trading normally. Fairfax House was to be built to the left of the pedestrian in the foreground.

Opposite below: The same corner as the previous picture, although the Briton's building has been demolished allowing a view of City Motors Garage in Quakers' Friars. The white van in front of the garage belongs to A.J. Phippen Ltd, wholesale grocers, who traded in Earl Street (near the present day bus station).

A similar view of Briton's corner, where building of the modern shops has begun – the road is devoid of all cars except for a single Ford Consul.

Broad Weir to Lower Castle Street. To the far right is the Bristol Co-operative Society building, education department. The advertising hoardings back on to Castle Green area where the houses of Middle Terrace can be seen in the left distance. The new shops in Lower Castle Street form the backdrop.

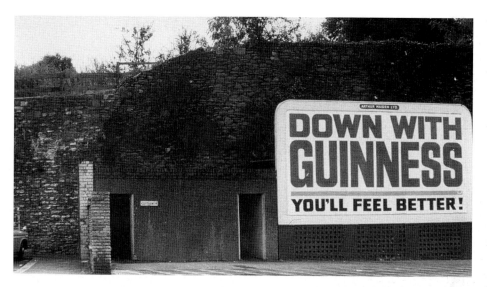

Broad Weir – can it be coincidence that the Guinness advertisement is next to the gentlemen's toilets?

Broad Weir from the Castle Green area looking up towards Merchant Street (off top right) and one of Fry's chimneys which is just visible in the distance. A barrow boy sells his goods as an Austin Devon pickup passes by. Early preparation has been made for demolition of these buildings – the tiles have been removed from the roof of No.15. The shop fronts have been boarded up and the windows are in disarray. This general view shows Elliott's, timber merchants, at No.17. The Gem Electric Theatre was built in what is now a gap (by the two advertising hoardings). To the right of this, W.H. Vowles & Sons, with the four arched ground floor windows, ran the Eagle Brush Works.

Left: Number 17 Broad Weir, was Elliot's timber merchants with its attractive brick frontage and Dutch gable giving a date of what appears to be 1889. One of their Bedford lorries is parked outside.

Below: Number 18 Broad Weir was the Old Crown public house. The Austin van on the left belongs to Mills & Rockley, outdoor advertisers of Lower Park Row and the van on the right to Priest & Reed, chain makers of Feeder Road.

Opposite above: Broad Weir showing the site of the Gem Electric Theatre and Robert's upholsterers, which is boarded up and awaiting demolition, late 1950s. The hoardings advertise Nestlé's Milk and Cerebos Salt being held by Philip Harben, one of the first television cooks. The car is a modern Ford Popular.

Opposite below: Number 15 Broad Weir, seen here in the centre, with six windows, late 1950s. In the 1920s it was a fish shop, and alongside it was a passageway that lead to Gabriel's Court behind. The shop on the left, No.16, is the appropriately named John Caines & Son, basket makers. The archway to the far left was the entrance to the Friends' Meeting House in Quakers' Friars.

Broad Weir, seen here when the modern shops of uniform frontages were nearing completion and which replace Elliot's and other early eighteenth–and nineteenth-century buildings, *c.* 1960. The tall crane rises above the building of Fairfax House.

Broad Weir from the lower Castle Street junction and Newgate, which was once Narrow Wine Street, in the distance, *c.* 1963. The shops, including the new Sainsbury's, gleam brightly.

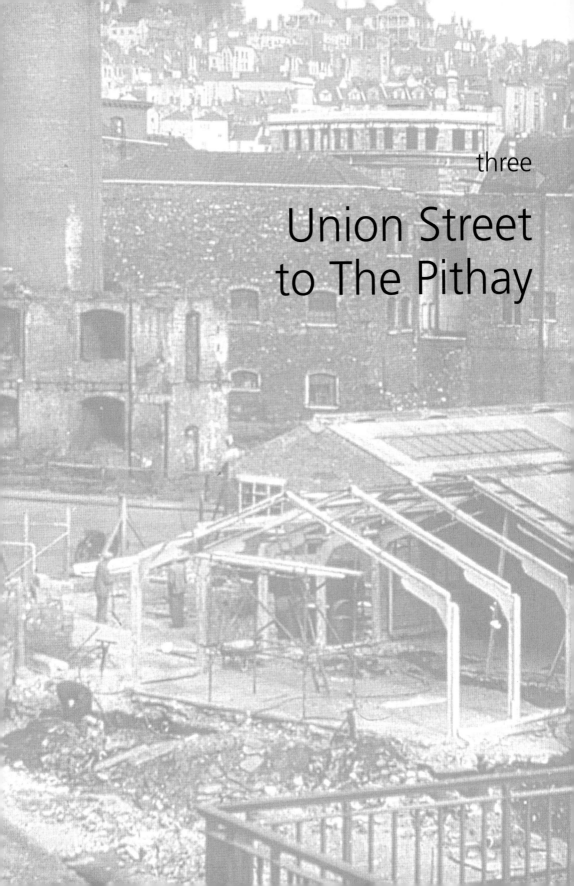

three

Union Street
to The Pithay

Having retraced our steps along Broad Weir to the castle area, we now start at the top of Union Street and descend the slope towards the Haymarket and back into the Pithay.

Union Street is built on made-up ground, it is not a natural slope. The road was laid out in the mid-1700s and early occupation was mainly by businesses, e.g. Ferris', druggists and Fry's chocolate manufactory. Fry's purchased the patents for cocoa-making from Walter Churchman of Narrow Wine Street in 1728 and went on to become a massive employer and to take over much of the area, to the west of Union Street, for their factories and offices. They operated one of the earliest steam-engines for manufacturing purposes in Bristol and expanded their business in 1840, building many new premises. This happened again in 1860 and 1876 when much of the Pithay area was bought up.

Towards the end of the nineteenth century terraces of housing in All Saints Lane and Wellington Street were demolished for yet more factories. It is not recorded what happened to the numerous occupants of these houses – they probably moved into shared accommodation, which then became badly overcrowded.

A very large meat market with fruit and vegetable market combined occupied the east side of Union Street. This gave way to more modern shops in the 1930s but some of the building lasted until the 1950s, although it was badly bombed. Today the site is occupied by the Galleries Shopping Centre.

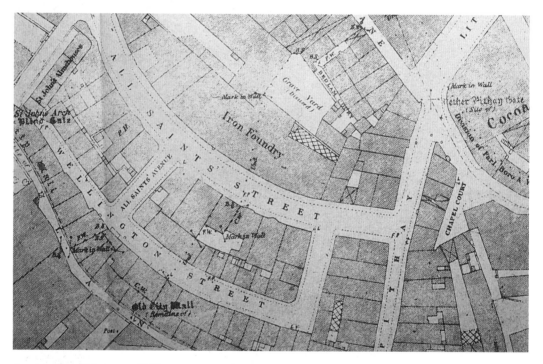

A map of the Pithay area, 1882.

Opposite below: Small shops in the frontage of what was once the very large St James' Market (this can just be made out in the stonework above the left-hand archway) in Union Street, 1937. The market had been there a long time and was rebuilt in 1858-59. The upper part was mainly a wholesale meat market – the rest was for cheese, vegetables and so on. Market days were Wednesdays and Saturdays. The doorway is approximately on the same site as an entrance to the Galleries Shopping Centre is today.

A view of Union Street bridge where the last reinforced concrete beams used to form the roadway are in position and ready to be lifted into place, 1953.

The row of shops between the market site and the Broadmead junction, Union Street, 1937. They are – from the right – Smart's, house furnishers, Bristol Wireless, Parker's bakeries and Harrold's, milliners. The steelwork in the foreground is for the construction of a new office block on the site of what was J.S. Fry's.

Union Street 1936-7. A view across the demolished Fry's building, which was to become the site of the Odeon, to the shops on the Broadmead junction. Broadmead Wireless, Palais-des-Fleurs, florists, and Clarke's, milliner's were all situated there.

The remains of the shops bombed nearly ten years after the end of the Second World War, but they all seem to be trading successfully, Union Street, July 1953.

The magnificent Fry's offices built in 1895, just prior to demolition to make way for the Odeon cinema.

Looking back up Union Street, *c.* 1936. Some of the old Fry's offices and factory are still to be demolished. In the foreground is the site where the Odeon would be built. Fry's business has been temporarily removed to the corner of Horsefair and Lewins Mead.

The Galleries Shopping Centre from Union Street bridge on the site of the old meat market, 2004. The architect appears to have been influenced by the frontage of the old buildings, as he has completed his with semi-circular and triangular detailing as well.

Lower Union Street. Between Broadmead junction and Haymarket was the very large Broadmead Baptist church. The Haymarket Hotel is on the far left.

The Haymarket Tavern (or Hotel) on the corner of Lower Union Street and Haymarket, February 1954. Two shops have been demolished and the site of Broadmead Baptist church is off to the right The back of the old houses are in the Horsefair and the spire of the Welsh Baptist church awaits removal.

Looking back up Lower Union Street and Union Street from the Haymarket to St Peter's church, 1953. These buildings are visible, as Fairfax House is yet to be built in front. Demolition is yet to start behind the Haymarket Tavern. The statue is of Samuel Morley, seen in his new position having been relocated from the Baldwin Street/High Street junction. He was an MP who represented Bristol for the Liberal Party in 1868 and 1874. He ran a firm of wholesale hosiers in Nottingham. The large shop at which he is looking is Pike & Tucker's, at Nos 55-57, corn merchants and animal feed makers.

Pike & Tucker's shop at Nos 55-57 Lower Union Street. The window is full of boxes of Nutrive Oblongs – puppy biscuits and meat and dog cake.

Union Street seen here where all the old buildings have been demolished and replaced by plain Bath stone, flat-faced, uniform frontages, 1960. St Peter's church is now obscured by a partially completed Fairfax House. The Odeon is showing *The Brides of Dracula* with Peter Cushing and the street is open in both directions for traffic.

Union Street is now one-way for vehicles and the road has been narrowed and trees planted, 1988. Pedestrianisation of the area, to make the shopping centre more 'shopper friendly', has begun. Fairfax House and all the shops on that side would soon be demolished for the Galleries Shopping Centre.

Right: Saunders, builders, is situated behind the two men on the corner of All Saints Street and All Saints Avenue, right, seen here in the late 1880s. Demolition of these houses had also begun – they back on to those behind the men in the archway in the Wellington Street photograph, below. Off to the left was a massive iron foundry belonging to Gardiner Sons & Co.

Below: Wellington Street, between All Saints Street and Tower Lane, was a road of eighteenth- and early nineteenth-century houses that were cleared away for a new Fry's factory. Demolition of the houses behind the men to the far left had already started at this time (late 1880s) and the signs on the walls read Fry's Cocoa. The curve of the street reflects the plan of the old city wall off to the right.

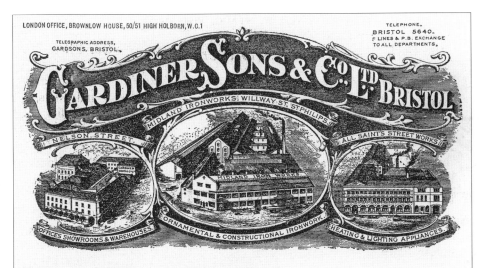

Above: An advertisement for Gardiner's showing the factory in All Saints Street and their nearby offices in Nelson Street.

Right: An ancient, probably half-timbered, house in the Pithay area. The lady in the foreground is filling a large pot from the communal pump, possibly having just washed the yard down.

Left: A drawing of the steps leading up from the Pithay to Union Street, alongside the River Frome, which was yet to be arched over. The overhanging property in the foreground is built above a semi-circular bastion on the old city outer wall. Union Street appears to have tall houses on both sides.

Below: The top of the steps from Pithay to Union Street are seen here in 1936. The bracket over the archway, which appears to have Ferris' name on it, has lost its gas lamp. In the wall just to the left of the door is a boundary marker of St Peter's parish, the exact boundary would be directly over the centre of the River Frome below. Fry's factory can be seen beyond the steps, in All Saints Street.

Opposite above: Looking back at the Pithay area from Union Street towards the demolished Fry's factory in Duck Lane and Little James Back, 1937. The building on the right, in the foreground, with two windows visible, is Bridewell police station.

A view from Union Street to the partially demolished Fry's factory shows the exposed base of one of their large chimneys.

An advertisement for Ferris & Co., Union Street.

four
Broadmead

Broadmead from Nelson Street to Merchants Street, always appears to have had a wide variety of shops and businesses. Probably the earliest trade known to have been carried on here was the making of broad-cloth or *brod-mede*.

The Cotterell brothers, around 1843, opened a manufactory for producing wallpaper here and until this date, paper was only made in comparatively short lengths and then stuck together. It also had a government duty imposed upon it making it very expensive. Once the tax was lifted Cotterell's, with their method of producing long lengths of patterned wallpaper at lower cost, were able to expand to become one of the major wallpaper concerns in the country, and they exported to the colonies and India.

The name of John Hall & Sons was prominent in Broadmead until they were bombed in 1940, although they kept a small shop there until the 1950s. The business began in 1788 when John Hall was apprenticed as a glazier, but he also made and sold paint and putty. The firm was the originator of brilliant cut glass and they received a gold medal for this at the Great Exhibition of 1851 in London. Their showroom was lit by a number of large stained glass windows and one of brilliant cut glass.

Alsop's house furnishers, who started their business around 1820, had a large furniture factory which fronted onto Broadmead and were very successful because they introduced steam-powered machinery for cutting timber.

At Nos 36 and 37 Broadmead on the corner of the Old King Street, Henry Jones had his patented flour manufactory, which allowed bread to remain edible for much longer than previously possible. The firm gradually grew and properties in the Old King Street were bought, demolished and rebuilt to allow the firm to expand.

The Odeon cinema on the corner of Broadmead and Union Street is well known and one of the only few left in Bristol. What is less well celebrated is that Broadmead can also lay claim to a tiny music hall, which was the first in Bristol, in 1896, to show moving pictures. This was The Star, later to be renamed The Tivoli, which had 300 seats. This wasn't a success and it closed a few years later, but became the Wellington Palace and finally The Broadmead before closing completely in 1936.

Broadmead could also boast two important early chapels. The Baptist Chapel, originally built in 1631 was rebuilt in the eighteenth century, and enlarged again before being remodelled in 1881. The second, which fortunately still survives from 1739 is John Wesley's first Methodist Chapel in Bristol – The New Rooms.

One of Bristol's first post offices was established next to the Greyhound Hotel, which was an important old coaching inn, but was sadly destroyed for the new shopping development in the 1950s.

Of all the streets engulfed by and changed for the new shopping centre, Broadmead itself has probably retained the most interesting buildings. Apart from the Greyhound Hotel, now only a façade serving as an entrance to the Galleries Shopping Centre, and Wesley's New Rooms there is also the Lower Arcade. This enclosed area of small shops was designed and built by James Foster in 1825, and was a rare survivor, unlike the Upper Arcade, of both bombs and planners, and serves to break up the uniform post-war street scene that is Broadmead today.

Opposite above: A well-known postcard of Broadmead, which is useful for showing the original complete north rank of shops from the Union Street junction, 1882. The photographer was where the Odeon was to be built some fifty years later. The flooding of 1882 was probably the most severe Bristol had for a long time and it is a reminder of the closeness of the River Frome and the possible origin of the name of this area – Broadmead – a wide meadow. On the left was a chemist shop, Edwin Harris and next Hone & Co., bulb and seed merchants. The low flat arch just below S. Jenkins is the entrance to the Baptist Chapel. These façades were to remain largely intact until demolition for the post-Second World War development.

Above: The same rank of shops as in the above picture showing Strode, Cosh & Penfold, chemists and truss makers on the corner of Lower Union Street and Hone's, still next door, during early 1951. However, further along the rank (above the lady crossing the road) the first gaps have appeared as demolition has started. This was the first set of buildings to disappear in the area to be replaced here by the new Marks & Spencer. The commissionaire on the right has probably come out from the Odeon (off to the right). All roads ran in both directions and an expensive pre-war saloon car – a Rolls Royce or Daimler – is parked alongside the entrance to Broadmead Baptist Chapel.

A view from the incomplete new Woolworths building showing Strode, Cosh & Penfold, to the right of the bus negotiating the tight corner into Lower Union Street, 1952. To the left of the bus is the other part of Broadmead with James Phillips & Sons, household furnishers, advertising Oriental carpets and linoleum. Far right is the entrance to Broadmead Baptist Chapel – a date of 1640 above the door. The road has been dug up, for new services to be laid.

February 1953. A close-up of the same rank, but Hone's has now become Parsons and Hone. Hobart's were manufacturers of food preparing machinery and Smart's are home furnishers – the scaffolding is for the building of Marks & Spencer. and Freeman, Hardy and Willis.

The demolition of the Broadmead shops has produced a vista across Horsefair to St James' Barton, 1951. The shops, including Palmer's bicycles, behind the steam shovel, are in St James' Churchyard (see p. 81). The spire belongs to the Welsh Baptist church.

Strode, Cosh & Penfold, Manfield's and the new Smart's are still incomplete, June 1954. The latter's new shop is approximately on their old site and Broadmead is now one-way for traffic.

October 1954. All the old and interesting frontages and shops have been demolished and rebuilt in this post-war uniform style. Burtons can be seen in the distance and Marks & Spencer, the tallest building next door, opened in 1952. Freeman, Hardy and Willis is on the near side of Marks & Spencer. All shops are complete and open for business.

The north side of Broadmead viewed from Merchant Street, c. 1951. The bus hides the bottom entrance to the Lower Arcade and the two arches to the right lead to the New Rooms, which was built in 1739, the first of John Wesley's chapels in Bristol. Jones' flour, right, is on the corner of Old King Street and next to that, the Armada public house.

Pianos are advertised at Bruton's, at No.33, to the left of the Antelope public house.

Jones' patent flour on the corner of Broadmead and Old King Street, July 1953. Henry Jones was granted a patent for his self-raising flour in 1845, which enabled bread to keep much longer than previously possible. The frontage is decked with window boxes and what can only be described as hanging troughs of flowers. The Antelope public house, is far left and Stokes the tobacconists and newsagents is the shop with the white blind.

The same view, but demolition has started on the Antelope. Other shops are closed and abandoned except for Jones' flour.

The Antelope and shops have gone, c. 1954. The new steelwork heralds the building of Jackson's tailors and the Lower Arcade is scaffolded in preparation for alterations.

The Burtons store is nearing completion, *c.* 1953. Marks & Spencer is still scaffolded and notice John Hall & Sons' tiny temporary shop. One of their vans is parked outside.

A look at the south side of Broadmead from Old King Street junction where Jones' flour 'towers above them all'– their emblem was a giraffe, 1954. Demolition has started on what, at the turn of the twentieth century, was Masters' Dining and Supper Rooms with the Rose and Crown on the corner already gone.
The steelwork, forms the beginnings of four similar semi-circular frontages built around the crossroads. The two vans on the left belong to Jones'. Above the front van the frontage of the Greyhound Hotel can just be made out. The tall chimney belongs to Fry's chocolate factory and the Odeon frontage is visible middle distance.

A similar view from further up Old King Street. The first of the Hub buildings, August 1955. Boots the Chemists and John Collier are both nearing completion. Jones' 'Bristol's Departmental Store' can be seen in Broadmead, as the sites of Jones' flour and the Armada have been cleared.

A Loxton drawing of the Greyhound Hotel, an old coaching inn, and to the right the double-gabled Broadmead post office, 1905. Bristol Tramways had their livery stables to the rear of these buildings.

Broadmead post office seen here around 1950 to '51. The planners wanted to demolish both the post office and the Greyhound Hotel for the new development but the latter managed to hang on, although only as a façade, until the present day.

The needless demolition of Broadmead post office, April 1951.

The south side of Broadmead, showing Union Street to the right with the Odeon canopy just showing, October 1948. Buildings destroyed in the blitz were situated on the corner of Broadmead and Union Street and are where Partridge and Love, printers, Woolworths and Dorothy Perkins were to be built. Swears & Wells, furriers' were yet to arrive on the corner. The white building on the left, with the bay windows, is the Greyhound Hotel.

The south side of Broadmead from Union Street, March 1952. The Greyhound Hotel to the right of the lorry is covered in scaffolding. Above the same lorry the white building is Fred Morgan's in Merchant Street (see p. 68). The scaffolding in the foreground was for the construction of Dorothy Perkins, Dolcis, Hepworths and Wallis stores.

Above: A view across Broadmead towards the Odeon over the steelwork for Marks & Spencer, and Freeman, Hardy and Willis, 1952. A Baldwins' coal lorry overtakes a horse and cart – a mix of the new and the old. Between them – with the clock – is an incomplete H. Samuel, jewellers. The steelwork to the right is that of Woolworths' front entrance.

Left: A view looking down to Wallis and Hepworth's stores, next to the saved Greyhound Hotel, July 1955. Broadmead post office appears to have been temporarily relocated in the shop, far left, next to the gap.

H. Samuel is practically completed, 1953. Woolworth's with its modern frontage is about to open. The roadmenders are still using a horse and cart for haulage and a manual, very heavy, road roller.

Woolworths' hoardings erected in readiness for demolition and the building of the Galleries Shopping Centre, 1988. The Odeon now has several screens and is showing *Three Men and a Baby* with Tom Selleck, and *The Last Emperor*.

five

Merchant Street, Old King Street and Barrs Street

These three streets together form the major north-west, south-east route across the area. The most southerly, Merchant Street is the only one, from Broad Weir to Broadmead, to retain its original name today, but in 1480 it was called Marshall Street, as it represented the main route from Bristol Castle to Gloucester.

Merchant Street has another of the old, saved buildings – the Merchant Tailors' Almshouses which were built in 1701. It is now incorporated into part of the Galleries Shopping Centre and has recently served as a bank. Again, this old building helps to relieve the monotony of the street scene.

A look at the *Kelly's Directory* of 1929 seems to show that for some reason Merchant Street was a magnet for house furnishing outlets, with Smith's, Jenkins' Day's, Olpin's, Bristol Furnishing Co. and Miles' all trading there.

Today the 'new' shops from the 1960s' redevelopment are beginning to show their age, and many are empty or only available on very short leases pending the latest plans to overhaul shopping in Broadmead.

Old King Street, across the junction with Broadmead, formed the next hundred yards or so of the road north to its meeting with the Horsefair. However, in this short street there were two of the largest chapels. The older one, Ebenezer Methodist with seating for nearly 1,000 people, was built in 1795 at the Horsefair end. On the opposite side, the slightly smaller and more recent Baptist Chapel was erected in 1815 – the date proudly displayed high on its classical frontage. The street can also boast at one time two public houses and an old forge and smithy, the latter only removed for the new-build in the mid-1950s. Old King Street is now only recalled in a short dead-end alleyway behind the shops, as the main thoroughfare of Old King Street now forms part of Merchant Street.

Barrs Street, north of the Old King Street intersection with Horsefair, to North Street, Stokes Croft, has completely disappeared. All its buildings and houses were demolished and the road itself excavated for the construction of Jones' store (now Debenhams). It was known as Barrs Lane as far back as 1129 when it was noted for having a pound and 'two great barns'.

Today Barrs Court, a tiny service road off the Horsefair, is all there is to remind us of this lost street.

Merchant Street,
Broadmead to Broad Weir.
[Parish—St. Paul.
1. Smith Arth. house furnisher
2, 3, 4, 48 & 49 Jenkins E. & E. ltd. house furnishers
5 Higgs Hubert Geo. dining rms.

6 Lenton J. & Sons,sheet metal wrkrs.
7 & 8 Day E. H. & Sons, house furnishers
——Quaker's Friars intersects
10 Harris Herbt. H. dining rms.
11 Olpin Hy. furniture dlr.
12 Vicary Wm. T. house furnisher
Holley Eli Courtney, *Merchants' Arms*, beer retailer
14 & 15 Bristol Furnishing Co.
16 to 20 Evans Brothers, wholesale provision merchants
——Quaker's Friars intersects
9 Olpin Hy. furniture dlr.
8 Brown F. F. & Co. hat mfrs.
7a Davies, J. hairdresser
6 Coombs & Co. sign writers

Turner J. W. *Mail Coach*, vic.
Street Mrs Kate, confectnr.
Church Hy. Edwd. newsagt.
here cross over
1, 2, 3 & 4 Miles J. K. house furnshr.
——*Fairfax Street intersects*
[Parish—St. Paul.
Winter J. H. & Co. electrical engineers
38 Hill Jonathan & Co. timber mers
Partridge & Love,limited, printers
41 Marsh Mrs Eliza, wardrobe dlr.
Weights & Measures Office—E. T. Thomas, inspector
42 Fox Mrs Ida, bird & animal dealer
43 Cabinet Makers Supply Co. timber mers.
44 Miller, Hunter & Co. upholsterers' warehsmn.
45 Pinney & Sons, bedding manufactrs
46 & 47 Pole Albert & Son (1914), ltd. printers
48 & 49 Jenkins E. & E. ltd. house furnishers
50 Peters Mrs Ada, tobacconist

Old King Street.
Broadmead to Barrs Street.
[Parish—St. James.
1, 3 & 5 Jones Henry (Bristol), ltd. patent flour manufacturers
7 Broad & Macadam (Jas. Brand F.R.C.V.S.propr.),veterinary surgns
9 Radford & Co. (H. Pratten,propr.), shoeing forge

11 Phillips James & Sons, limited, furniture removers
15 Dickson Frederick J. greengrocer
17 Britton Sidney Robert, hair dresser
19 Gordon Geo. & Son, ltd. printers
23 Tonkin John, gramophone dealer
25 Richards Joseph, fruiterer
WESLEYAN METHODIST CHAPEL
27 Stokes John, pawnbroker
27 Cook Alfred D.
here cross over
[Parish—St. Paul.
18 Waycott Bros. motor engineers
14 & 16 Colston Furniture Manufac- turing Co. furniture manufacts
12 Newick Henry C. soap dealer
10 Parker Sidney Herbert & Son, glass merchants
BAPTIST CHAPEL
8 Adams Antiques, antique furniture dlrs.
6 Emery Thos. boot repr.
6 Holmes Edwd.
4 Matthews Henry & Co. limited, oil manufacturers
2 Cotton M. ltd. cabnt. ironmngrs.

Barrs Street,
Old King Street to North Street.
[Parish—St. Paul.
1 Nash Philip, shoe maker
2 James Mrs Dorothy, draper
3 May Mrs Marion, milliner
4 & 5 May Stacey Wm. dining rms.
6 Epstein & Co. picture frame mkrs
8 Cottrell Fred, saddler
9 Rogerson Mrs Clara L. tobccnst.
10 Willey & Co. timber merchants
11 Colledge T. & Son, leathr. fctrs.
BARRS COURT.
1 Stone Samuel
2 Millard Miss Clara
3 Bicker Mrs Harriet

12 Barton Wireless & Electrical Sup- ply (The), wireless dlrs.
13 & 14 Scully Joseph & Sons, printers
15 Fisher Charles & Co. wine & spirit merchants
here cross over
[Parish—St. James.
16, 17, 18, 19 & 20 —The Barton Ware- houses. Lim.
21, 22 & 23 Cottrell's, china and glass warehouse
21 & 22 Cottrell William, ladder maker Smith Thos. *White Horse Hotel*,vict.
Gardner Ernest H. carrier

Left: Entries from *Kelly's Directory*, 1929.

Opposite below: This view shows Jay's shop, which was between Castle Mill Street and Fairfax Street. The Bristol Co-op hardware department was next door Behind the lamp post is the Merchant Tailors' Almshouses. Which was the Weights and Measures office in the 1920s. The man unloading the Bedford van is outside W.D. Church, the newsagent.

64

Castle Mill Street to Merchant Street, 1957. Jay's shop seen below, would have been on the site behind the boarding near the lorry (about to turn into Broad Weir). Briton's, furnishers, on the corner can be seen above the lorry. The massive warehouse used by Burleighs', printers, is visible above the shops, in Quakers' Friars. St Paul's church, in Portland Square is just showing above new shop building.

Fairfax Street and Merchant Street corner, where Millets was to be built, on the site in the foreground. Jay's old site, seen here to the right, was to be occupied by Fairfax House. The Merchant Street shops opposite include Coombs and Salanson.

Fairfax House seen here taking shape. Millets is now completed and in business, 1960-61.

Merchant Street again, with Briton's shop on the far right. Jennings, wine merchants, is advertising Loch Dee Blue Label Scotch Whisky. The Mail Coach public house is on the left, and is the same building occupied by Salanson on the previous page.

Merchant Street, showing the Mail Coach to the right, then Coombs, sign writers, Jay's, fireplace shop; Pictons, opticians workshop (main shop as seen in Union Street) and J. Olpin empty for imminent demolition.

Merchant Street, showing J. Olpin's shop to the right and the entrance to Quakers' Friars. Evans Bros, wholesale grocers, with a load of sacks and boxes awaiting delivery from a Morris commercial lorry belonging to Tilly's, & Sons of Barton Hill.

Merchant Street from Broadmead. To the extreme right are Evans Bros wholesale grocers; then the Merchants' Arms and another entrance to Quakers' Friars; a timber suppliers and Fred Morgan's, home furnishers, facing on to Broadmead. Off to the left is Rosemary Street.

Merchant Street, 1930s. The demolished building to the left of Fred Morgan's, seen previously, is also on the left in this photograph; then Arthur Smith's, another house furnisher, on the corner of Rosemary Street. The building on the right, in Broadmead, was the Rose and Crown.

The whole rank of buildings from Fred Morgan's to Evans Bros, has gone and has been rebuilt. Olpin's is just hanging on for a few more months.

Old King Street. Jones' flour factory is on the corner of Broadmead, left and Fred Morgan's is on the corner diagonally opposite. T. Deas, clothiers, is to the right on the corner of Rosemary Street, next to Henry Matthews, oil manufacturers along with Rogers', printers, and Rouch & Penny, electrical engineers. The Hoover lorry outside is probably collecting mended electric motors or delivering them for repair. The double decker is a No. 2 on its way to Eastville. The steelwork behind the lamp post is for the new Jones' department store.

The Baptist chapel, built in 1815, is next to Rouch & Penny, to the right, and was demolished for the building of the British Home Stores.

Old King Street on the far side of the crossroads with Fred Morgan's shop (end of Merchant Street) just visible. The car is almost in front of the Baptist Chapel which is tucked behind the shop frontages, but just visible above them. Waycott's, motorcycle dealers, adjoining Ridley's Almshouses were advertised as being 'of international fame' and are seen here on the corner of Milk Street. Barrs Street is in the foreground.

Old King Street with Waycott's, 'motorcycle experts' to the left, Newick, soap dealers and Parker, glass merchants, to the right, above which can be seen the top of the Baptist Chapel. The road name sign is an interesting glimpse into what is to come, as the Old King Street is about to disappear; it reads Merchant Street, formerly Old King Street..

Opposite Waycott's shop (just visible to the left) was the Methodist chapel with seating for 900 people. To the right of the church is The Clock Shop on the corner of Horsefair.

On the same side to the left of the chapel – the portico just visible above the car, a Wolseley, – was this interesting group of buildings, seen here in June 1953. In the foreground Jones' flour manufactory and then a tiny, half-timbered, doubled-gabled property behind which was a shoeing forge.

In 1905 Loxton drew these frontages, but at that time there were six gables. The forge was through the high square doorway.

In 1906 the six gables had been reduced to four by the demolition of the nearer two for an extension to Jones' flour manufactory, left, with their giraffe emblem. The forge was owned then by Radford & Co.

Right: A close-up of the forge frontage, now owned by E.D. Hart, but specialising, not in shoeing horses, but producing and retempering vehicle springs, 1953.

Below: Barratts and Past Times occupy the site of the old forge, shops and Methodist church, 2004.

Left: A view looking up Old King Street, foreground, shows the Baptist Chapel has yet to be demolished, left. Some old shops in Merchant Street are still standing. The new Hub building is under way on the site of Fred Morgan's shop, to the top left of the roundabout and Broadmead is off to the right.

Below: Merchant Street now, but it used to be Old King Street, Waycott's shop would have occupied the site above the gas-lit 'Turn Right' sign. The 1815 Baptist Chapel was where the tall, incomplete BHS building can be seen on the right.

Barrs Street was a continuation, across the junction, of Old King Street. The Clock Shop would have been on the corner far left, and Ridley's Almshouses on the right. The tall houses are in St James' Barton. The street was completely lost for the building of Debenhams (or Jones' as it was initially known).

The excavated site of Barrs Street in the foreground. Looking into Old King Street, past the Clock Shop on the right, on the corner with Horsefair, the Wesleyan Methodist Chapel's roof is visible above. Waycott's motorcycle shop is on the other corner but Ridley's Alshouses are no longer there.

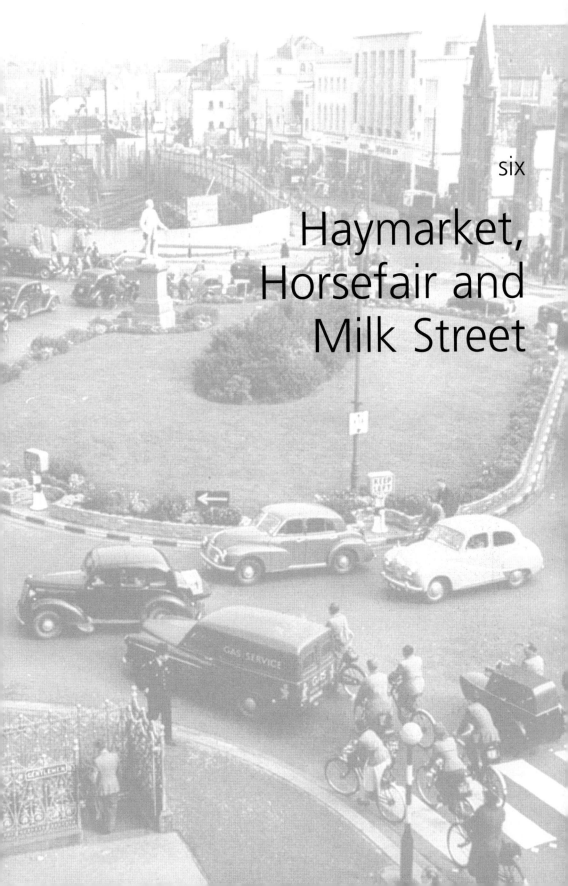

six

Haymarket,
Horsefair and
Milk Street

This part of the walk is from what is now House of Fraser and Debenhams, into a street which has now completely disappeared – Milk Street. In 1480 it was called Kings Street. The site of House of Fraser (built as Lewis's) was once that of the St James' Fair held annually in July. It was really a trade fair with manufacturers coming from the north with their wares to sell. It was abolished on 16 July 1838.

The building of Lower Union Street in the 1860s caused the demolition of the Chequers Inn, Horsefair, which derived its name from the items with which the merchants used to do their accountancy.

St James' churchyard was taken over by the local authority and became a playground in June 1882, being welcomed by the local population. There was a fountain and a weighbridge, the latter continuing a tradition from 1785 when magistrates erected a weighing machine to check weights of items sold at the fair.

Horsefair clearly indicates another use for the open land here, but the street had many shops, as well as the entrances to Upper and Lower Arcades. Behind many of these shop-frontages were the courts of houses that could be entered by a passageway, often with its own door to the street. These early eighteenth- and nineteenth-century houses had very poor natural light and ventilation, and were frequently very overcrowded even as late as the 1930s when they disappeared through the slum-clearance schemes.

The shops in Horsefair were removed for early redevelopment of the shopping centre. Marks & Spencer, Lewis's (opened in September 1958) and Jones' (1957) were built instead. Thomas Jones, a draper opened a shop in Wine Street in 1843, but the Blitz took its toll on the business, which later recovered as one of the first of the new development. Debenhams now occupies that site.

Milk Street was the continuation of Horsefair, across Old King Street. It was a quaint, busy and mixed shopping area, with businesses, churches and hidden housing. As early as 1775 Bence Lockier & Woodward imported mahogany to a yard in Milk Street. Later Mardon, Son & Hall made paper bags and had a printing business, and W. Summers made and bottled mineral waters. The Clarke's business here was a very large clothing wholesalers.

Milk Street is probably remembered by many for Ridley's Almshouses near Old King Street and the tiny, early nineteenth-century watchman's hut outside. Sarah Ridley left £2,200 in 1726 for an Almshouse for '5 old bachelors and 5 old maids' to be built and stipulated that occupants should neither be married nor Roman Catholic. Regrettably, Ridley's Almshouses and the Milk Street name were lost.

Opposite above: The Haymarket roundabout with the statue of Samuel Morley MP, who has his back to Bond Street, *c.* 1950. On the right is Horsefair. The park is the site of St James' churchyard and the row of shops behind the trees was named after it.

Opposite middle: Horsefair from the Haymarket roundabout, *c.* 1950. The little building on the left is a weighbridge. The bus has stopped near the junction with St James' Churchyard and the white shop on the corner was Fred Palmer's cycle shop. Above the bus the roof of the Methodist church in Old King Street can be seen. To the far right the Haymarket Tavern is in view, then Charles Stephens, hairdresser and Broadmead Chapel entrance. The P.O.P. to the right of the bus is an advertisement for Oliver Pragnell Ltd, paint makers at No.16 Horsefair. The letters stand for: Pragnell's Own Paints.

Opposite below: Haymarket to Horsefair, showing Lewins Mead brewery in the distance, *c.* 1950. Stephens' hairdressers and Mrs Ponting's dining rooms have had their upper windows removed prior to demolition. The archway next door is the entrance to Broadmead Chapel and the church on the left is Broadmead Baptist Sunday school.

Above: A view across the park beyond the weighbridge. The white gabled building to the left is Frederick Roberts' typewriter shop. An interesting study in black and white: the shops, the kerbs around the islands, the keep left signs, the Belisha beacon poles, the no-entry sign poles and the zebra crossing.

Left: St James' Churchyard showing two old half-timbered buildings: the typewriter shop and the Carpenters' Arms. Bond Street is off to the left.

Opposite below: The White Lion and Palmer's cycle shop, showing Horsefair off to the right, June 1953.

Looking up St James' Churchyard from Horsefair to Bond Street. Demolition has begun, next to the White Lion, right.

View across the park. The weighbridge and fountain remain for a short while longer. All the buildings in St James' Churchyard, from the Carpenters' Arms right down to Palmer's cycle shop have disappeared – the street line is indicated by the fence in the middle distance. St James' Barton, top, is in the far distance.

Looking across the site of demolished buildings in St James' Churchyard. Excavation has begun, revealing the mass graves of victims of the plague. Lewis's was to be built here. Horsefair is behind the lorry and is still mostly intact.

A traffic jam, *c.* 1955 Buses indicating Nos 2, 3 and 5 negotiate the path between the cars. Excavation of Lewis's site is well advanced. A great deal of Horsefair has been swept away and the new Marks & Spencer, the gleaming white building, has taken the place of those previously demolished.

The clearance of the St James' churchyard site allows a vista from St James' Barton left across North Street, Stokes Croft to St James' Square and Milk Street.

The view is now obscured by the steelwork for Lewis's and Jones' new department stores.

Lewis's takes shape, as the Portland stone cladding is put in place, *c.*1957. Bond Street has been newly widened in the approach to Stokes Croft – the roundabout has been laid out – before it was altered to the sunken 'bear pit'.

Above: Horsefair. The north side looking towards Barrs Street corner. The lower end of the Upper Arcade had been badly damaged by bombing and behind the row of buildings between Norris and Bowerman and the White Horse Hotel were two areas of housing, Jarman's Court and Reynards Place. PHY 208 is a Hillman Minx.

Left: Reynard's Place, drawn by Loxton in 1905. The passage, a mere three-and-a-half feet wide, leads to Horsefair. There were four houses here and a total of fourteen people were displaced when the properties were subjected to slum clearance in 1935.

Demolition of the shops has begun, including the site of Reynard's Place. Milk Street is seen in the distance, 1953.

The rank of buildings from Norris and Bowerman to the Barrs Street corner, including the White Horse Hotel, now gone forever, November 1953.

Horsefair to Barrs Street corner, to the left in the picture, with the White Horse Hotel, which would have been to the left of the pedestrians; Milk Street is in the distance, November 1953. The Clock Shop to the right is on the corner of Old King Street and is also the pawnbrokers. Milk Street is in the distance and Ridley's Almshouses are just visible, right, beyond The Clock Shop.

The south side of Horsefair , where Onion's French polishers were situated. Behind these buildings, entered by a small door and a tunnel, were St Stephen's Court and Wesley Court, two very enclosed groups of houses tucked out of the way and invisible to the general passer-by. Off Wesley Court was another enclosed court, i.e. one which was accessed and exited by the same route, called Pim's Court. In the distance is the new Marks & Spencer.

Opposite: Pim's Court consisted of four properties, in which lived a total of nineteen people, in each family paying rent of about 4s, 1932. There were no flushing toilets and the water supply was a communal one in the yard outside. The occupants had no washing facilities, the windows and floors were rotten, the roofs leaked and the walls were badly decayed and damp. The buildings were pulled down in 1933 as part of the slum-clearance scheme and the notice requiring this to be done can be seen on the wall above the bath tub. A magnificent gas lamp lights the court.

Right: A map of the Pim's Court area, 1882.

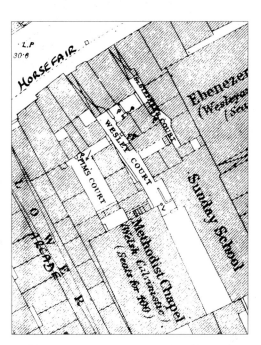

Milk Street, a continuation of Horsefair, beyond the junction with Barrs Street, left, and Old King Street, right. The incomplete name near the pawnbroker's sign is that of Hardware (Bristol) Ltd, wholesalers of glass and chinaware. Between them and the crossroads was Ridley's Almshouses and opposite Clarke's, clothiers. The site with the hoarding to the extreme left was that of the Plume of Feathers public house, as seen in the following photograph.

A similar view of Milk Street, in 1906 when the area around the Plume of Feathers was vibrant and in its heyday. To the left, can be seen the shop of Radford, saddle and harness maker, who also had the shoeing forge in Old King Street. R. Clarke's massive clothing factory rises behind and the two large white towers, belonging to the Methodist Chapel, are above the gentleman on the pavement, far right. The White Horse Hotel is on the far left.

November 1953. View from Milk Street back into Horsefair with Clarkes' factory site shrouded in scaffolding waiting for the bulldozers to move in. Behind the traffic lights would once have stood the White Horse Hotel.

The north side of Milk Street looking out of town, June 1953. The rusticated archway, extreme
left, is one of the towers belonging to the Methodist church. The street is intact and quaint. A little
Austin rumbles towards Horsefair. The strange dustbin-like feature to the right on the wall is an
advertising sign for A.H. Day, tin-plate maker, which was incorporated into the business of Hardware
(Bristol) Ltd. The shop with the blind pulled out is Weare's, butchers, and immediately beyond this,
the car park sign is pointing up St James' Square Avenue to St James' Square. On the other side of
this lane is the Crown and Cushion public house.

Clearance has
begun on Milk
Street and a tower
belonging to the
Methodist church
has been reduced
to a single storey.
Further demoliton
to the church, out
of view, is attracting
a crowd.

Another crowd is fascinated as the main body of the Methodist church is destroyed. This is the view from the end of Horsefair.

Milk Street seen here with St James' Square Avenue, off to the left. A better view of A.H. Day's tea-urn advertising sign is on the right. Cherry Alley is off to the left, just behind the pedestrians; a small, hemmed-in lane with four tiny houses. There were seven people living in No.1 and nine in No.3. All properties were removed in July 1936 having been declared unfit for human habitation. The traffic lights are at the junction with York Street, left.

A good view of the Crown and Cushion and shops, revealed because of the demolition of the buildings on the other side of the road. An Austin Devon saloon sits on the waste ground.

Newfoundland Street was a continuation of Milk Street, and today leads out to the M32 motorway, but is seen here in March 1954. Clark Street is off to the right, and Mills Place, to the left. Mills Place comprised eight houses in a cul-de-sac, each three storeys high, but with sink and water closets in the open yard. Thirty-one people were displaced when the houses were cleared away in 1935, during slum-clearance.

Milk Street, looking back towards Horsefair from the crossroads of York Street to the right and Leek Lane on the left, with the Lamb and Anchor on the corner. In the middle distance, left, by the Nescafé advertising hoarding, is the old coaching-yard entrance.

The Lamb and Anchor from York Street, with Leek Lane and the Merchant Venturers' Technical College just in view, to the left.

Percy Green's sweet shop, right, is next to the old coaching-yard entrance, and was soon to be razed to the ground. An Austin Big Six is parked with the Lamb and Anchor behind.

The Lamb and Anchor, is to the far left and Colston Place is through the archway between the Favourite Café at No.16 and the shop with the lovely bow-fronted windows, probably dating from the early 1800s. The old coaching yard is by the lamp-post.

Milk Street is seen here from the old coaching-yard entrance looking towards Horsefair in the distance. To the left of the man pulling the cart is the entrance to Colston Place. Colston Place was a group of seven little houses declared unfit for habitation and condemned in 1938. The two magnificent towers of the Methodist Chapel can be seen in the distance. St James' Square is off to the right, behind the Crown and Cushion.

Opposite above: Demolition of the Lamb and Anchor is under way. The shops in Milk Street have already met their fate, as have the buildings in Leek Lane by the road-roller to the left.

Right: Milk Street where the No.84 bus from Hotwells slipped on the icy road surface and crashed into the garage belonging to Hardware (Bristol) Ltd causing serious structural damage. The photographer was stood outside Ridley's Almshouses to capture this picture.

Below: The flattened site of Ridley's Almshouses from Old King Street looking across Milk Street to the Surrey Lodge, Brunswick Square (to the left of the tree) and the remains of the east side of St James' Square, above the car.

A view from Horsefair to Milk Street, in the distance, above the cars. Dunn's shop has appeared on the right, approximately on the site of the Clock Shop. Ridley's Almshouses would have been on the corner, above the keep left sign, 1957.

Ridley's Almshouses corner, September 1960 where rebuilding continues apace. A white Ford Zephyr comes down what was Milk Street.

seven

St James'
Square

St James' Square was started in 1707, around the same time as the Tailors' Almshouses in Merchant Street, but unlike that building, was badly damaged during the Second World War. The final blow was then administered by the planners in 1970, when the remaining houses were demolished for the building of Avon House North. The square could only be entered by vehicles from the south via a little lane, St James' Square Avenue, which connected it with Milk Street.

The square was built well away from the squalor and smells of the city, and consisted of nearly twenty, substantial five-storey brick-built houses. Only the well-off could afford to purchase a property there.

One such was Richard Reynolds, a Quaker, who was an iron-master, after Abraham Darby, at Colbrookdale in Shropshire. A plaque erected in his memory can just be made out on the photograph of the northern range of buildings.

It reads: 'In memory of Richard Reynolds distinguished philanthropist and benefactor to the poor. Born in Bristol on 1st November 1735 and died 10th September 1816. Interred in the Friends Burial Ground. Resided here 1804 to 1816'.

Next door lived Sarah Champion from another famous Quaker family. She bought the house in January 1794 for £600 (quite a considerable sum then) plus an extra £200 for the fixtures and fittings. She lived there until February 1802 when she sold it to Dr Thomas Pole.

Other influential people who resided there in the late eighteenth century were Isaac Baugh, alderman and merchant and George Daubeny, sugar refiner.

Between the houses on the west side of the quare and Barrs Street lay the YMCA hall, which was regularly used for lectures and meetings. One such meeting is covered later in the chapter.

As quite often happens to the large properties, like those being discussed, the houses in St James' Square began to fall from grace as they were expensive to run. They were divided up and let out to several families and little money was spent on their upkeep. Certainly by the beginning of the twentieth century the tenants were mainly commercial businesses, not residential, and when repairs proved too expensive, cheaper options like removing architectural detailing, such as the pediment on the east block, took place instead. As early as 1864, the firm of Vowles, organ builders were employing as many as fifty people in one of the properties.

Despite its very run-down appearance by the 1960s, some buildings could have been saved to compliment the other squares nearby, Portland Square and Brunswick Square.

Regent Terrace to the south west of the square, 1953. Already in a state of disrepair, the middle two properties have lost their mansard roofs. To the far left one of the towers of the Methodist Chapel in Milk Street can be seen from the rear.

Vehicles could only enter or leave the square by the narrow roadway on the south side via St James' Square Avenue, leading down to Milk Street. Even during the 1930s the houses were falling into disrepair. The building behind the car may have suffered fire damage and appears close to complete collapse. Off to the right was a small row of six houses, entered by the south-west corner called Regent Terrace and is seen in the previous picture.

A similar view but from a height, above Stokes Croft, 1950s. All the houses on the south and west sides have been pulled down. Regent Terrace would have been to the right-hand side in the middle distance. The site of the seemingly fire-damaged house, seen in the top picture, now has a commercial garage trading there.

The east side of the square, still pretty well intact, including most of its original architectural features, is viewed from the entrance to Regent Terrace, c. 1932. In the diagonally opposite corner behind the attractive gas lamp is the small lane leading to St James' Terrace, again a cul-de-sac. To the left of this passage the Bristol Button Works and E. Cratchley, tailor, advertise over the doorway.

The east terrace is falling into disrepair and windows are boarded up or missing, 1953. Most properties there at that time were hardware or cutlery distributors. Victor J. Biss, wholesale stationers and A.C. Hobbs, dealers in paper, twine, cutlery and tools, shared a premises. To their left is Basire Bros, sheet metal workers. Note that the decorative central pediment at roof level, which appears in the above photograph, and which should be seen over Westhill's premises, has now been completely removed giving a rather plain and odd look to the terrace, not helped by the removal of the chimneys and dormer windows.

The north side of the square is seen on the left in this picture, with a good range of 1930s and '50s vehicles – probably taken on a weekday. The foreground wasteland was once the site of beautiful Georgian houses.

The north side again – probably taken on a weekend, as there is only one car in view. The terrace is now called Roydon House within which both Roydon's and Jackson's manufactured clothing. Also advertised are G. Heavers selling items for the hairdressing industry. To the left of the central doorway between the two windows the eagle-eyed may notice a plaque. This is to celebrate the fact that Richard Reynolds lived here from 1804-16. In the foreground the western terrace and the YMCA building have been pulled down.

The north-west corner is, architecturally intact. The road setts are laid out to decorative effect around the central gas lamp. Ralph Allen occupies this site, trading as a wholesale clothier before Roydon's take over. Especially noteworthy is the wonderfully complete dentilled cornice below the dormer windows, much of this detail was to disappear at a later date during modernisation. The passageway between the two terraces leads to Stokes Croft, *c.* 1932.

The same north-west corner, the west terrace has gone giving views across the empty site to St James' Barton and the Royal Fort.

MR. R. HENRY JONES, M.Sc., F.C.S.

Conference,

Feb. 5th, 1910.

Y.M.C.A.,

Bristol.

Above and below: Henry Jones gave a talk at the YMCA in St James' Square on the dangers of smoking – especially for children. He was speaking out about smoking saying that 'a cigarette in a boy's mouth shows his moral deterioration and he is, or soon will be, a moral and physical wreck'. He was quite advanced in his thinking, it would appear, in that he questioned the habit of smoking from the chemical effect it had on the blood, mentioning nicotine in particular. He also stated that smoking caused cancer, but when questioned, could not say why exactly, but he went on to say that passive smoking could also be dangerous to health.

THE ..
Young People's Anti=Smoking League.

ESTABLISHED 1898.   Head=quarters—Y.M.C.A., BRISTOL.

The President *and Committee invite*..
and a Friend to meet R. HENRY JONES, Esq., M.Sc., F.C.S., &c., in

═══ Conference, ═══

on Saturday, February 5th, in the LECTURE HALL of the Y.M.C.A.,
St. James's Square, Bristol.

Mr. JONES, who is Head of the Chemical Department, Harris Institute, Preston, will give an Illustrated Lecture, on "THE PROBLEM OF SCHOOLBOY SMOKING from a hitherto-neglected standpoint," and invites free discussion at its close.

Demonstration—Mr. JAMES PHILLIPS, B.H.U.   Discussion opened by Dr. MORGAN.

 CHAIR WILL BE TAKEN AT **7** O'CLOCK BY
GEORGE T. COOKE, Esq.
RECEPTION AND REFRESHMENTS at **6** till **6.45** p.m.

Kindly notify your acceptance or otherwise not later than February 1st to Rev. WILLIAM MAYO, Hon. Sec., 44, Sefton Park, Bristol.

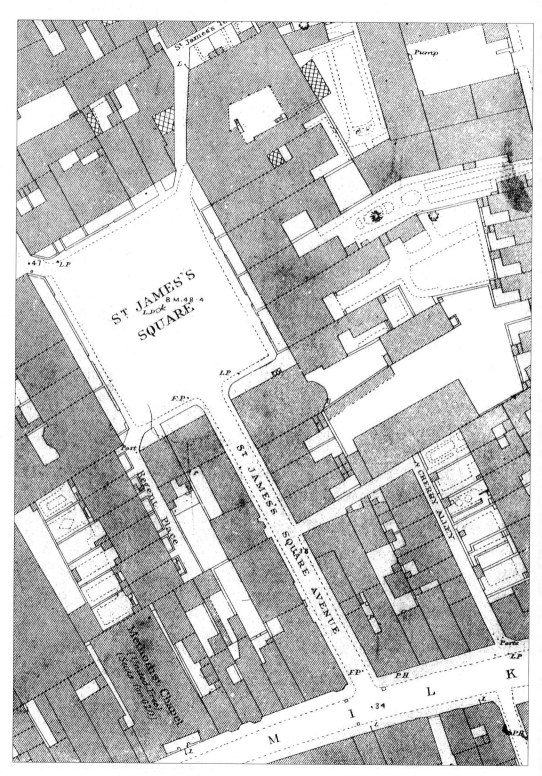

A map of St James' Square in 1882.

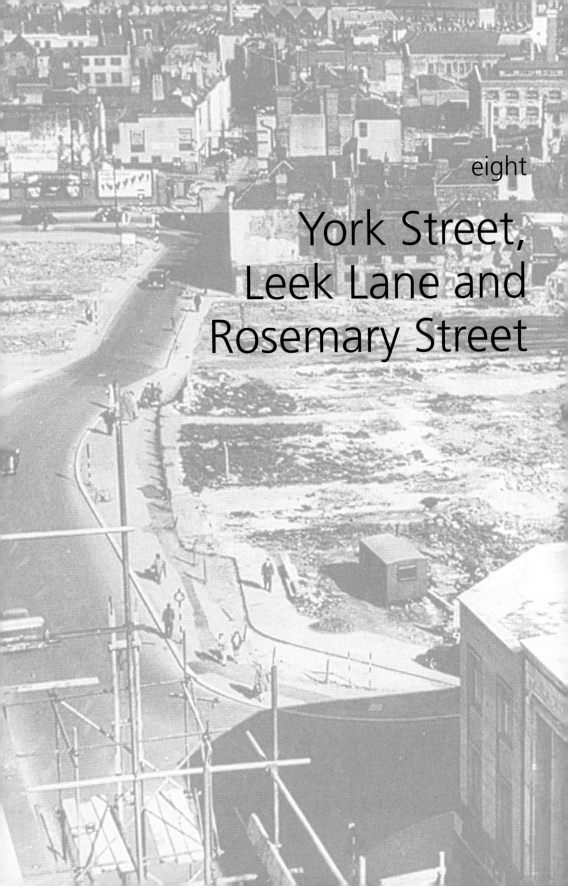

eight

York Street, Leek Lane and Rosemary Street

This chapter takes the reader from the southern part of Brunswick Square, which fortunately still remains, down to York Street across Milk Street to Leek Lane and right into Rosemary Street.

York Street was probably built as infill between the large new houses in Brunswick Square and the old little houses in Milk Street, in the latter part of the eighteenth century. It was quite a short street with modest two- and three-storey properties abutting the pavement with no gardens. By the end of the nineteenth century, many of these had become commercial premises and others demolished to allow similar developments.

In 1928, for example, there was a boot and shoe sewer, The Colston Clothing Co. and the Ashley Vale Biscuit Co. as well as G.C. King's, and Hansford's the mineral water bottlers.

The York Street name is still retained today for the very short length of road between Brunswick Square and the dual carriageway.

The name and the obvious position of Leek Lane has completely disappeared from the map since the shopping centre was built. Much of one side of the street was occupied by the Lamb and Anchor, which fronted Milk Street, and the other side had two large brick buildings belonging to the Merchant Venturers' College.

Callowhill Street, off Leek Lane was once occupied by the Asylum for the Blind in the latter seven years of the eighteenth century. It appeared to rely on sales of basketware and donations to boxes, as well as legacies, for survival. The accounts for 1799 show that their turnover for the year amounted to over £600, and that about twenty people occupied the premises. It was felt that if more money could be raised, a larger building could be purchased and up to fifty blind people could be helped.

At the end of Leek Lane was Rosemary Street, which was really just a narrower continuation of Broadmead. Even as late as the redevelopment, Rosemary Street remained with a cobbled surface and was lined with ancient gabled houses and hidden courts.

Opposite above: York Street, March 1954. The west side, from Brunswick Square to Milk Street which can be seen in the distance and the tall building is the Lamb and Anchor public house. It appears that some of these early nineteenth-century brick houses have been altered. The opening up of their frontages to form access ways for horses and carts allowed the use of land behind for commercial purposes. The large archway with the white surround is the entrance to G.C. King's and Hansford's, both mineral water bottlers. King's advertising emblem on their bottles was of a Mr Pickwick figure holding a lemonade bottle. Between King's and Milk Street, the original properties had been replaced partly by a three-storey building that housed the Ashley Vale Biscuit Co.

Opposite middle: Leek Lane. The east side, looking up to Milk Street where a Bedford lorry heads into town, towards the end of York Street down which the bus has come, September 1955. The Merchant Venturers' College workshops are on the right, on the corner of Callowhill Street. The car is an Austin A55.

Opposite below: The cars sweep down York Street across Milk Street and into Leek Lane towards the Merchant Venturers' workshops, on the left in the distance, March 1956. The Lamb and Anchor was probably rebuilt and enlarged around 1900 as the 1883 map shows it with a much narrower, and bayed, frontage. The sign at the start of Leek Lane advises that Rosemary Street is closed and the alternative route into the centre is along Milk Street.

The college's frontage on Callowhill Street, September 1955. This building replaced the Beaufort Iron Foundry and a large boot and shoe factory. Before, in 1793, the Asylum for the Blind was built here.

The blind school or Asylum for the Blind, 1793.

Above: The Merchant Venturers' College of Technology in Leek Lane, between Callowhill Street and Water Street, to the right. A large public house used to be here on this corner before being replaced for H.W. Twiggs' pram factory. Their painted name is just distinguishable above the top windows. The college workshops building on the corner of Callowhill Street is just visible top left.

Left: An Austin pickup, on its way down Leek Lane, passes the Lamb and Anchor, September 1955. The tall houses to the extreme right are in Brunswick Square; the smaller ones in York Street, where the Ashley Vale Biscuit Co. premises have completely disappeared.

The lower part of Leek Lane looking at the junction with Rosemary Street, along which the couple push their pram towards town, February 1954. Frank Onion had his French polishing business at No.3 and Ferris', druggists, were adjoined to the Lamb and Anchor at No.7. Passageways, one with the low flat arched frontage, led to York Buildings (where ten little houses were situated around a small, dark, gas-lit court) and Kingston Place.

Rosemary Street looking towards Broadmead in the distance with Leek Lane off to the right and Philadelphia Street, to the left, July 1953. The street surface is of stone setts, the larger flat stones, at the junction with Leek Lane, form a road crossing, which was regularly cleaned of horse droppings and mud, by the crossing sweeper so that the ladies' long skirts would not become dirty. The Friends' Meeting House (Quakers' Friars) is to the left of the Humber car driving into the centre and opposite was another workshop building of the Merchant Venturers' College, which appears to have been reduced to one storey from four in this picture. It was built after the removal of Ruffet's Court.

Rosemary Street as before, but the south side, including the gateway to the Friends' Meeting House, Quakers' Friars, has gone as has most of the north side. Only the little shop on the corner with Leek Lane right, remains to provide a location marker for this scene. Quakers' Friars is off left; Marks & Spencer is visible behind the little Austin A35 estate. The old stone setts and pennant paving is being removed for the new street line, which is to be called Broadmead.

A similar view, but showing gabled seventeenth-century houses, looking very run down, which belonged to the Bristol Municipal Charities in the foreground, July 1953. The doorway closest to the camera opened on to a passageway to five little cottages called Broad's Court. One of the tenants, in 1906, was a Samuel Radford, possibly a relation of the saddler or blacksmith in Barrs Street and Old King Street. Another was William Huxtable, coach builder in No.6 with his wife and daughter who later, as an old age pensioner, was removed from here when the cottage was declared unfit in 1937. It was a true back-to-back house, with No.5 Colston Place behind.

Rosemary Street – north side towards Leek Lane and the Merchant Venturers' College. The remains of the large building on the left are those of the Merchant Venturers' workshop. The railings on the right indicate the position of the Friends' Meeting House gateway seen below.

The south side of Rosemary Street from outside the gateway to the Friends' Meeting House (Quakers' Friars), which is now the Register Office, to the junction with Philadelphia Street, April 1953.

All properties have been demolished in Rosemary Street allowing a view of the back of the 1815 Baptist Chapel in Old King Street, *c.* 1953. Leek Lane, is to the right and Philadelphia Street to the left, but it is now called Penn Street. In the distance the new Lewis's and Jones' department stores are nearly finished.

The south side of Rosemary Street, *c.* 1957. The ancient buildings of the Dominican monastery far left fortunately survive, as the columns of the new shops begin to rise.

The junction of what was Rosemary Street, foreground, and Old King Street and Merchant Street. Phase four of the Hub building begins to take shape so that British Home Stores can start to construct their shop on the site of the old chapel.

A view from the top of Lewis's across the flattened cityscape of Milk Street, seen here to the left and Old King Street, which is in the foreground, c. 1957. The line of Rosemary Street can be seen running off diagonally to the right. Penn Street Tabernacle is to the far right in the distance. York Street, where this chapter began, is top left where the two cars are approaching the Milk Street junction with Leek Lane.

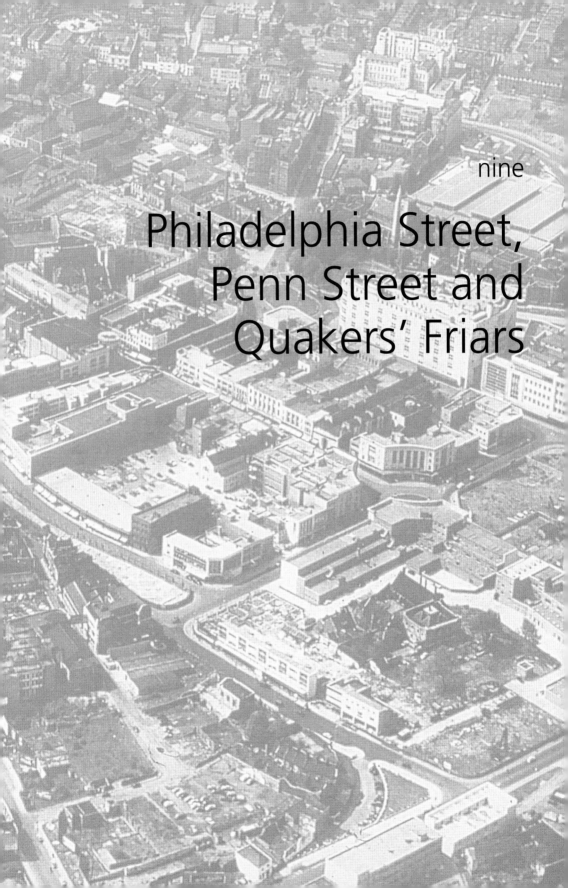

nine

Philadelphia Street, Penn Street and Quakers' Friars

In this final chapter we look at Philadelphia Street, Penn Street and Quakers' Friars whose names, along with Callowhill Street and Hollister Street nearby, were all interlinked by Quaker family connections.

William Penn Junior became a very wealthy man because Charles II was indebted to William's late father and granted him nearly 50,000 square miles of territory in America in 1681. William named this after his father and it became Pennsylvania, with its capital Philadelphia. He was the governor from 1682 to '84.

William later returned to Bristol and married Hannah Callowhill in 1696 in Quakers' Friars. However, before she had married Thomas Callowhill, who was a rich merchant, she was Hannah Hollister.

Her father, Dennis Hollister, another wealthy merchant and MP had not only purchased the old friary buildings, but he later sold an area of land to William Penn Jnr on which to lay out streets and to build houses.

A glimpse at these streets on the old maps shows that they appear completely different to the ones we have previously looked at. Instead of buildings of all ages and sizes where the old had been demolished and rebuilt, where houses mixed with shops, where little businesses existed in back streets and alleyways, there are dead straight lines only of houses.

These streets were planned on a green-field site, with all the houses built at the same time and to a similar size.

Initially the houses would have been sold or let to the wealthier people, but time takes its toll and they each became divided up and let out to several families, perhaps each occupying one floor. By the late nineteenth century they had become very poor accommodation and were included in the slum-clearance schemes of the 1930s. At some stage, some of the houses had their gardens built on to provide more, sub-standard housing, and hence you had Tabernacle Row squeezed in between Penn Street and Philadelphia Street.

Even cursory research into these houses indicates why they had to be torn down and the occupants rehoused. Probably the worst was No.23 Philadelphia Street. In this three-storey house plus basement, lived twenty-four people, including a family of ten with only three rooms, one of which had no window for light or ventilation. The shared water supply for all occupants was a tap over a sink in the yard next to the two shared unflushed WCs.

In one room, six people slept, but all the glass in the windows was broken, the frames rotten and a sheet of canvas kept out the wind. All the floors were badly destroyed due to woodworm, the roof leaked and the walls were crumbling. No wonder the surveyor wrote that it was unfit, but the owners still took £1 5s 2d a week in rent in total. They wrote to the council to say that the house was in good condition and fit enough for the 'poor class of people living there who were glad to have somewhere to stay'.

The slum clearance of the mid-1930s in the Philadelphia and Penn Street area caused the re-housing of over 340 families – more than 1,100 people. The surveyor summed up their homes precisely: 'The houses are absolutely worn out – their day is done'.

Opposite above: Philadelphia Street (right) from Rosemary Street with Penn Street parallel behind the buildings, September 1955. Water Street is across the junction and Leek Lane to the left with Twiggs' old pram factory on the corner. After this building was sold to the Merchant Venturers' College, Twigg's moved to the factory seen on the right. The corner shop, just visible in the view (see also p114), is distinctive for its 'acorns' on the roof and was Henry Sergeant's, the undertakers. The gap to the right was once No.35 Philadelphia Street, a house of three storeys in which lived thirteen people with a shared water closet in the rear yard. The house occupants, the slum clearance inspector noted, had no readily available water supply; he declared it unfit and it was demolished in 1934.

Middle: Philadelphia Street looking towards Narrow Weir and the terraces of houses on Castle Green. The last remaining original houses at this end of the street belong to the firm of Yeadon Adnitt and have survived because they could not, being industrial premises, be cleared when the slums were pulled down. In No.24, furthest from the camera, were four families, three living in two rooms each, the other in only one and paying 2s 6d a week for the privilege. The factory buildings near the lorry were constructed after the slums were cleared away, but they themselves were only to last twenty years. The buildings belonged to James, cabinet makers.

Right: Looking along Philadelphia Street from Castle Green. The building on the right was James, cabinet makers and opposite was the cardboard box manufactory of White & Sons. The Guinness advertisement is approximately on the site of what was the Black Boy, beer retailer, in Narrow Weir.

Looking down old Penn Street towards Narrow Weir with the end wall of Fred Morgan's, furnishers, in the newly built shops in Lower Castle Street, a continuation today of the re-aligned Penn Street, September 1955. On the extreme left is the Seven Stars public house, with Cross Street behind, leading to Hollister Street. Beyond is the Tabernacle with the adjoining Sunday School. This view shows how narrow the street was – the three-storey houses that existed on both sides must have let in little sunlight to the houses opposite.

Above: Numbers 6 and 7 Penn Street with the Tabernacle on the right. Typical of the houses in the street, but they were not included in the slum-clearance scheme. They were pulled down when everything else went, in order to prepare for the new Broadmead Shopping Centre.

Right: The Seven Stars as seen on the corner of Cross Street, off to the right, October 1955.

Opposite below: Penn Street looking back to the Seven Stars in the distance, April 1953. The Sunday school is in the foreground with Whitfield's (Penn Street) Tabernacle behind. Adjoining the yard on the right was Island Court, five small houses in a hemmed-in courtyard approached by a covered passage only 5 ft wide. Twenty-six people were moved out when the dwellings were pulled down after being denounced as unfit in 1934.

Penn Street, on the opposite side to the Tabernacle, October 1955. This is the back entrance to the premises of Yeadon Adnitt in Philadelphia Street. It shows how some of the original houses have been adapted and re-used for commercial purposes.

The bus is about to enter new Penn Street, which is more on the line now of Philadelphia Street, which has disappeared. The bus has come down what was approximately Leek Lane, York Street is in the foreground and Milk Street, off to the right. The C&A shop is now Primark.

Penn Street from Lower Castle Street, 1961. Broad Weir is off to the left. The modern shops are not quite complete and are yet to be let. The bus approaches the junction with what was Rosemary Street. The one-way system has yet to be thought of.

City Motors, Quakers' Friars. It is hard to believe that a commercial garage of this importance could exist tucked away behind the old shops and houses. This view is only possible by the removal of the buildings in Merchant Street and Broad Weir.

An aerial photograph of Broadmead, 1957.

An aerial photograph of Broadmead, 1959. Many of the buildings and shops seen in the previous photograph have gone and the new street alignments are noticeable.

Aerial photograph showing the 'hollow' centre of Quakers' Friars to be set aside for parking and dustbins, *c.* 1960. It also shows that the shop frontages are 'all for show'! Top right is the roundabout at the junction with Broadmead, with ex-Old King Street on the right; ex-Rosemary Street at the bottom and Merchant Street on the left. The tall buildings facing the roundabout have been referred to in this book as the Hub, as they represent the centre of the new post-war Broadmead development.

Other local titles published by Tempus

Around Stapleton

VERONICA SMITH

Illustrated with over 200 photographs, this pictorial history is a remarkable evocation of life in and around the Stapleton of yesteryear. From timeless vistas of the Frome Valley to snapshots of the bandstand at Eastville Park, local sporting heroes at Alexandra Park, Fishponds Lido and Coronation Day parties, this volume provides a nostalgic insight into the life and changing landscape of the area around Stapleton.

07524 3059 9

Castle Park: Before the Blitz

MAURICE BYE

This book records life in the area of Bristol known today as Castle Park before it was largely destroyed during a bombing raid on the night of 24 November 1940. Illustrated with over 150 archive images, this volume documents the streets and buildings, pubs and hotels, shops and local businesses of this once busy shopping area.

07524 2864 0

Haunted Bristol

SUE LE'QUEUX

This selection of newspaper reports and first-hand accounts recalls strange and spooky happenings in Bristol's ancient streets, churches, theatres and public houses. From paranormal manifestations at The Bristol Old Vic to the ghostly activity of a grey monk who is said to haunt Bristol's twelfth-century Cathedral, this spine-tingling collection of supernatural tales is sure to appeal to anyone interested in Bristol's haunted heritage.

07524 3300 8

Bristol Times *Revisited*

DAVID HARRISON

This book is a collection of some of the articles drawn from the first year of the *Bristol Times* supplement of the *Bristol Evening Post*. Each extract recalls an aspect of the city's lively, and sometimes turbulent, history. From tales of fairs, workhouses, riots and gaols, to accounts of star appearances at the hippodrome and the success of Fry's chocolate factory, each piece provides an insight into Bristol's past.

07524 2844 6

If you are interested in purchasing other books published by Tempus, or in case you have difficulty finding any Tempus books in your local bookshop, you can also place orders directly through our website

www.tempus-publishing.com